T0040040

Earth in Space

Glen Phelan

PICTURE CREDITS

Cover, page 25 (bottom left), Bettmann/Corbis; page 1, NASA; pages 2-3, Norbert Rosing/National Geographic; pages 6-7, 34 (bottom), Photographer's Choice/Getty Images; pages 10 (top), 17 (bottom right), 19 (bottom left), 25 (top right, bottom right), 26-27 (bottom), Royalty-Free Corbis; page 10 (bottom), Michael K. Nichols/National Geographic; page 13 (top left), The Image Bank/Getty Images; page 13 (bottom right), Michael S. Yamashita/Corbis; page 14-15 (all images), Jan Halaska/Photo Researchers, Inc.; page 16, LWA-JDC/Corbis; page 17 (top left), Eric and David Hosking/Corbis; pages 18, 20, 22, Richard Hamilton Smith/Corbis; page 19 (top right), Ralph A. Clevenger/Corbis; pages 21 (top left), 31 (bottom), 34 (center), Chase Swift/Corbis; pages 21 (bottom right), Dianna Sarto/Corbis; page 23 (left), Darrell Gulin/Corbis; page 23 (right), 36, Gary W. Carter/Corbis; pages 26-27 (top), Paul A. Souders/Corbis; page 28, Kenneth Seidelmann, U.S. Naval Observatory, and NASA; page 29, Rob Howard/Corbis; page 30 (top left), Altrendo/Getty Images; page 30 (top right), Ariel Skelley/Corbis; page 30 (bottom left), Brand X Pictures/Getty Images Royalty-Free; page 30, Photodisc Red/Getty Images Royalty-Free; page 32, Robert Harding World Imagery/Getty Images

Produced through the worldwide resources of the National Geographic Society, John M. Fahey, Jr., President and Chief Executive Officer; Gilbert M. Grosvenor, Chairman of the Board; Nina D. Hoffman, Executive Vice President and President, Books and Education Publishing Group.

PREPARED BY NATIONAL GEOGRAPHIC SCHOOL PUBLISHING

Ericka Markman, Senior Vice President and President, Children's Books and Education Publishing Group; Steve Mico, Senior Vice President, Editorial Director, Publisher; Francis Downey, Executive Editor; Richard Easby, Editorial Manager; Bea Jackson, Director of Layout and Design; Jim Hiscott, Design Manager; Cynthia Olson, Art Director; Margaret Sidlosky, Illustrations Director; Matt Wascavage, Manager of Publishing Services; Sean Philpotts, Jane Ponton, Production Managers; Ted Tucker, Production Specialist.

MANUFACTURING AND QUALITY CONTROL

Christopher A. Liedel, Chief Financial Officer; Phillip L. Schlosser, Director; Clifton M. Brown III, Manager

CONSULTANT AND REVIEWER

Priti P. Brahma, Ph.D., NOAA/NWS, Silver Spring, Maryland

BOOK DEVELOPMENT

Amy Sarver

BOOK DESIGN/PHOTO RESEARCH

3R1 Group, Inc.

◀ **The moon can be seen from the surface of Earth.**

Contents

Published by the National Geographic Society
1145 17th Street N.W.
Washington, D.C. 20036-4688

ISBN: 0-7922-5428-7

2010   2009   2008
   3 4 5 6 7 8 9 10 11 12 13 14 15

Printed in Canada.

Earth

Earth's Place in Space

Earth is one of eight planets that move around the sun. Other objects in space also move around the sun. The sun and everything that moves around it make up our **solar system.**

Look at the picture. It shows the sun and the planets in our solar system.

- How many planets move around the sun?
- How many planets are closer to the sun than Earth?
- How many planets are farther from the sun than Earth?

solar system – the sun and everything that moves around the sun

Big Idea
Earth's movement causes day, night, and seasons.

Set Purpose
Learn how Earth moves through space.

How Does

Questions You Will Explore

What causes night and day?
What causes seasons?

Earth Move?

Our world is full of movement. Birds fly through the air. Cars move along a road. But the planet we live on seems to stand still. Yet Earth is really moving. Our planet moves in two ways.

- Earth spins like a top.
- Earth moves around the sun.

In this book, you will learn more about the ways that Earth moves each day.

12:00 p.m.

7:00 a.m.

7:00 p.

▲ As Earth rotates, the sun seems to move through the sky.

Earth and the Sun

During the day, the sun seems to move. It looks like it moves across the sky. Yet the sun is not moving. Earth is!

Earth is always moving. Earth **rotates.** That means it spins around and around. You cannot feel Earth rotate because you are moving along with it. Yet it is always spinning in space.

rotate – to spin around

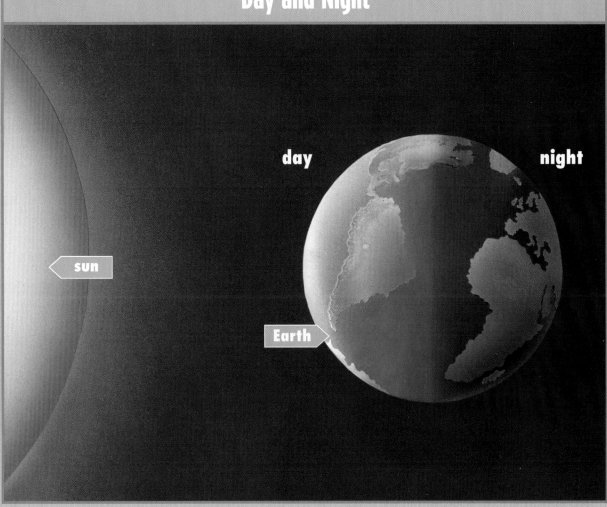

day   night

sun

Earth

▲ As Earth spins, one half of Earth has day and the other half has night.

Day and Night

Earth's spinning causes day and night. As Earth rotates, half of it faces the sun. Sunlight reaches this part of Earth. It is daytime. The other half of Earth is facing away from the sun. Sunlight does not reach this part of Earth. This half has night.

◄ In the morning, this city moves into the sunlight.

► In the evening, this city moves out of the sunlight.

Sunrise and Sunset

As Earth rotates, places on Earth move into and out of sunlight. At sunrise, the sun looks like it is moving up into the sky. You are on part of Earth that is turning toward the sun.

At sunset, the sun looks like it is moving down through the sky. Your part of Earth is turning farther away from the sun.

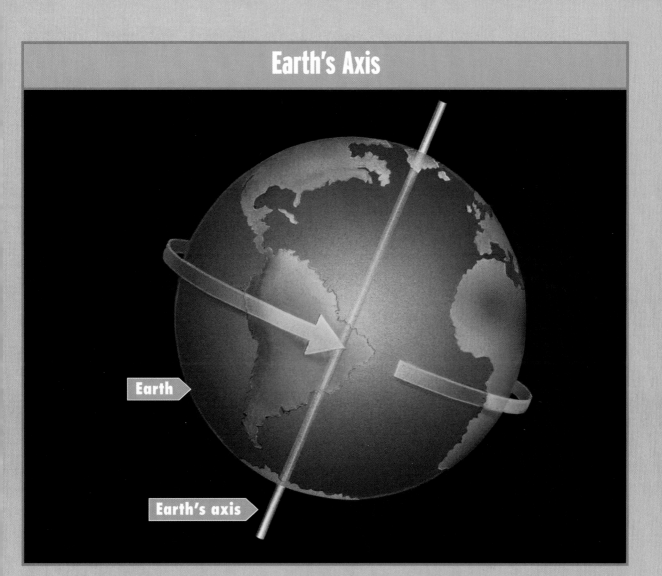

Earth

Earth's axis

▲ Earth spins around its tilted axis.

Earth's Axis

Earth rotates around its **axis**. Earth's axis is an imaginary line that runs through the center of Earth.

Earth's axis is not straight up and down. It is tilted. Earth's axis is always tilted the same way.

axis – an imaginary line around which an object rotates

Earth's Orbit

Spring: On March 21, the northern half of Earth begins to tilt toward the sun.

Winter: On December 21, the northern half of Earth is tilted farthest away from the sun.

sun

Summer: On June 21, the northern half of Earth is tilted most toward the sun.

Autumn: On September 21, the northern half of Earth begins to tilt away from the sun.

▲ Seasons change as Earth moves around the sun.

Earth's Path Around the Sun

Earth spins. But Earth also moves in another way. It **revolves,** or moves around the sun. Earth moves around the sun in a curved path. This path is called an **orbit.** It takes Earth 365 days to complete an orbit around the sun. That is one year.

You cannot feel Earth moving through space. Yet you know it is happening. You can see it in the seasons.

revolve – to move in a curved path around something

orbit – a curved path of one object around another object in space

▼ **Winter in New York City**

▲ **Summer in New York City**

Seasons

Each year has four seasons. They are spring, summer, autumn, and winter. Earth's tilt causes the seasons.

The northern part of Earth has summer when it is tilted toward the sun. At this time, the southern part of Earth has winter. The southern part of Earth is tilted away from the sun.

The northern part of Earth has winter when it is tilted away from the sun. At this time, the southern part of Earth has summer.

Stop and Think!

What causes day, night, and the seasons?

13

Recap
Explain why there are seasons on Earth.

Set Purpose
Learn how seasons cause changes in a park.

▲ Spring

▲ Summer

▲ Autumn

▶ Winter

The Changing Seasons

In spring, the tree is covered with tiny buds. The buds become leaves in summer. During autumn, the leaves turn bright orange. By winter, the leaves have all fallen off the tree. Each season brings changes. Let's take a look at how a city park in Minnesota changes during the year.

Spring

Spring

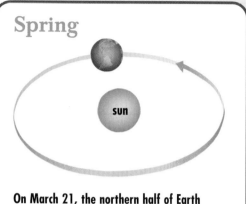

On March 21, the northern half of Earth begins to tilt toward the sun.

Spring in Minnesota

In spring, the park comes to life. Many changes are happening in Minnesota. Why? Today is March 21. It is the first day of spring. On this day, the northern half of Earth begins to tilt toward the sun. That means this part of Earth is getting warmer.

▼ These people hike through the park in spring.

▲ Birds and other kinds of animals have babies in spring.

Spring Flowers and Birthdays

During spring, the park gets warmer. Plants begin to grow. Tiny buds cover the trees. Cherry trees show their pink and white blooms. Wildflowers peek out of the ground.

Plants are not the only things coming to life in the park. Rabbits and squirrels have babies. Birds lay eggs. Soon the eggs will hatch, and more birds will live in the park.

▲ In spring, this cherry tree is covered with white blooms.

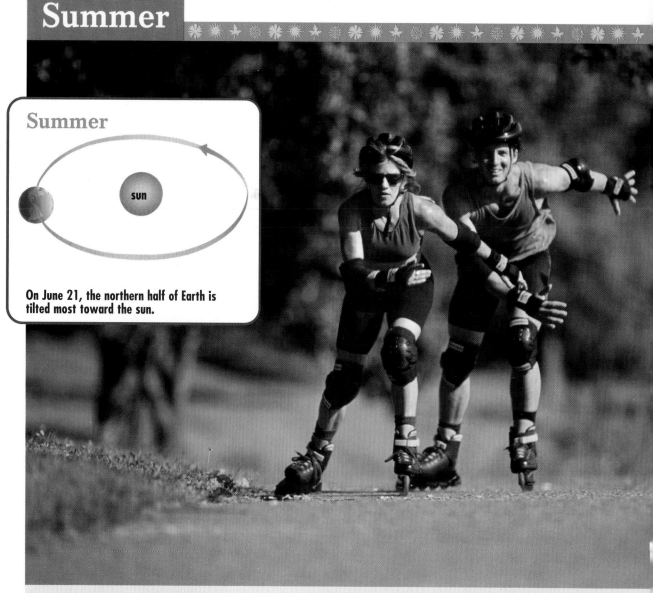

Summer

On June 21, the northern half of Earth is tilted most toward the sun.

▲ In summer, people skate through the park.

Summer Fun

In summer, the park is full of people. Some people have picnics. Others play games. It is hot and sunny in Minnesota. Today is June 21—the first day of summer. The northern part of Earth is now tilted toward the sun.

Trees, Bees, and Summer Heat

In summer, the park's trees are covered with green leaves. The grass is thick and green. Wildflowers bloom during the summer.

If you stop to smell the flowers, be careful. Bees fly from flower to flower. Mosquitoes fly in search of food. Crickets chirp. Insects are everywhere.

In summer, rabbits and squirrels lose their thick winter fur. They do not need thick fur in the hot summer.

▼ **In summer, bees travel from one flower to another.**

▼ **These wildflowers bloom in summer.**

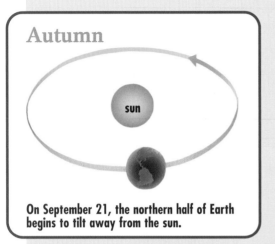

Autumn

On September 21, the northern half of Earth begins to tilt away from the sun.

Autumn Is Cool

As summer ends, there is less sunlight each day. But you are having too much fun to notice! In autumn, school starts. Today is September 21. This is the first day of autumn. The northern half of Earth starts to tilt away from the sun.

▼ **In autumn, the leaves of these trees change colors.**

◀ **Geese migrate during autumn.**

Autumn Leaves Are Falling Down

In the park, the trees are changing colors. They change from green to bright yellow, orange, and red.

Above the trees, there is another sign of autumn. A flock of geese is flying in a V-shape. These geese **migrate,** or move to another place. The geese are flying south to live in a warmer place during the winter.

▲ **This squirrel eats extra nuts in autumn.**

Many kinds of animals are getting ready for winter. Squirrels, rabbits, and other animals are eating a lot of extra food. They are getting fat. The extra fat will help them survive the coming winter.

....

migrate – to move from one place to another

Winter

On December 21, the northern half of Earth is tilted farthest away from the sun.

▶ This man skis on snow in winter.

Winter in the Park

In winter, the park is cold. It is December 21. Today is the first day of winter. The northern half of Earth is tilted farthest away from the sun.

Winter Wonderland

In the park, snow covers the ground. Snow also covers the trees. Everything looks white. Some people ski on the snow.

Winter is a cold time for animals in the park. Some animals, such as raccoons, grow thick winter fur. The park's birds grow extra feathers that help keep them warm.

As Earth moves around the sun, the seasons change. Each season brings changes to the park.

Stop and Think!

Why do seasons change?

▼ This raccoon grows thick fur in winter.

▶ These birds do not migrate during the winter.

Recap

Explain the changes that can take place each season in a park.

Set Purpose

Read these articles to learn more about how Earth moves.

Earth in Space

Earth is always moving. The movement of Earth causes day and night. It also causes the seasons.

Here are some ideas you learned about Earth as it moves in space.

- Earth rotates around a tilted axis.
- As Earth rotates, different places on Earth face the sun.
- Earth revolves around the sun.
- Earth's tilt causes seasons as Earth revolves around the sun.

Check What You Have Learned

What do the pictures show about how Earth moves?

▲ Earth rotates around its tilted axis.

▲ As Earth rotates, this city moves into and out of sunlight.

▲ Earth revolves around the sun.

▲ Autumn is a season caused by Earth's tilt and its movement around the sun.

Amazing Migrations

Birds are amazing! Some of them migrate thousands of miles each fall and spring. They fly back and forth to the same places each year. How do they find their way?

Scientists do not know for sure. But they think some birds use the positions of the sun and stars. Some might use landmarks, such as mountains, to guide them.

▶ **Geese migrate thousands of miles each year.**

Ancient Calendar

Thousands of years ago, these large stone blocks were placed in a circle. Some scientists think the stones formed a calendar. Long ago, people might have watched the sun rise over certain stones. This may have showed that a new season was beginning.

▶ **These stones might have been used to show the first day of each season.**

A Different Tilt

Not all planets are tilted like Earth. That is true for the planet Uranus. Uranus is the seventh planet from the sun. Its axis is so tilted that it rotates on its side as it moves around the sun. Uranus is the only planet in the solar system that is tilted like this.

This strange tilt gives Uranus very extreme seasons. During most of the year, the sun shines on one half of Uranus. This side of the planet is very hot, and the other half is very cold.

▼ Uranus is tilted on its side.

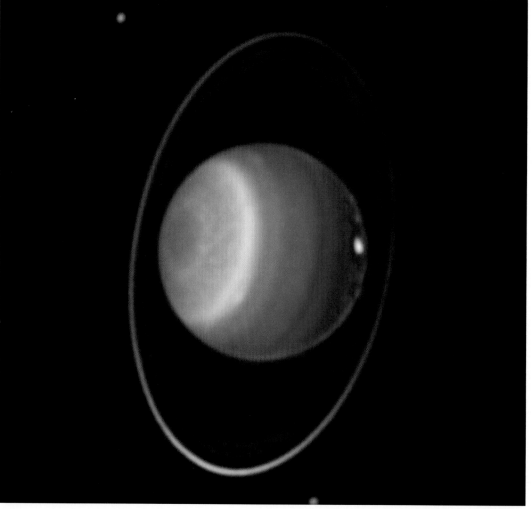

On some days of the year, the sun does not set in the Land of the Midnight Sun.

Land of the Midnight Sun

Did you know that there are some places on Earth where the sun does not set each day?

In the most northern places on Earth, the sun does not set for much of the summer. This area is called the Land of the Midnight Sun. The sun moves close to the horizon. But it never goes below it. It is like sleeping with a huge night-light on!

Many kinds of words are used in this book. Here you will learn about homophones. You will also learn about root words and derivatives.

Homophones

Homophones are words that sound alike but have different meanings. Find the homophones below. Then use each homophone in a new sentence.

The **sun** is bright.

Her **son** is five years old.

He said that he would meet her in two **hours.**

The coats are **ours.**

Root Words and Derivatives

Some words are root words. They can be used to make other words. A new word made from a root word is called a derivative. Look at these words. Use each in a new sentence.

Planets, such as Earth, **rotate.**

One **rotation** of Earth takes 24 hours.

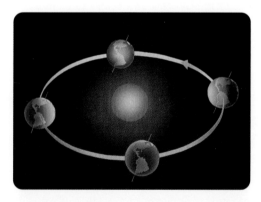

The planets **revolve** around the sun.

Earth's **revolution** takes 365 days.

In the fall, the birds **migrate** south.

The birds' **migration** can last a few weeks.

Research and Write

Write About Seasons

Research the seasons in a city you would like to visit. Find out how the seasons in that city compare to the seasons where you live. Then make a poster that shows what you learned.

Research

Collect books and reference materials, or go online.

Read and Take Notes

As you read, take notes and draw pictures.

Write

Make a poster that lists how the seasons in the two places are alike. Make pictures that show details about the seasons.

Read More About Earth and Space

Find and read other books about Earth and space. As you read, think about these questions.

- How does Earth compare to other planets in our solar system?
- What tools help people learn about planets and other objects in space?
- Why do scientists study space?

Books to Read

▲ Read about the relationship between Earth, the sun, and the moon.

▲ Read about how people explore space.

▲ Read about how people study space and the objects in it.

Glossary

KEY CONCEPT

axis (page 11)
An imaginary line around which an object rotates
Earth's axis is always tilted the same direction.

migrate (page 21)
To move from one place to another
Geese migrate twice each year.

KEY CONCEPT

orbit (page 12)
A curved path of one object around another
object in space
Earth's orbit curves around the sun.

revolve (page 12)
To move in a curved path around something
Earth revolves around the sun.

rotate (page 8)
To spin around
Earth rotates around its axis.

solar system (page 5)
The sun and everything that moves around the sun
Our solar system includes the planets that move
around the sun.

Index